XO 6352

'Swallow Sidecars built bodies for Austin Sevens that most definitely had ideas above their station. Swallow sidecars became SS, and of course after WW2 they changed their name to Jaguar'

The exquisite little blue cars from Molsheim won literally hundreds of races, including the first Monaco Grand Prix

Ettore Bugatti was an Italian who built the most celebrated cars ever to wear French racing blue. He was perhaps an artist first and an engineer second. Together with his son Jean, he produced what were quite simply some of the most fabulous automobiles ever made.

Ettore set up in the town of Molsheim in Alsace and began trading on 1st January, 1910. The town had been German, but after a war spent designing

Bugatti Type 35/35B

aero engines in Paris, Ettore returned to a French town. His successful Brescia model, based on the pre-war Type 13, became a respected racing car, with many victories to its name.

In 1922, Ettore designed the engine for the Type 30 – a 2.0-litre straight eight with one exhaust and two inlet valves per cylinder, driven by an overhead camshaft. In 1924, a development of this engine was used to power the new Type 35 competition car. It was a Grand Prix car, but had

two seats so that it was capable of carrying a riding mechanic.

Every detail was meticulously conceived, designed and manufactured. The aim was to save weight, but the result was an exquisite automobile. At a time when many cars ran on wooden wheels and sports cars all had wire wheels, Ettore created beautiful eight-spoke cast aluminium wheels, with integral brake drums. The engine was also a work of art, with a simple unadorned design.

The Type 35 was a huge success, and as it developed it became faster and faster. The Type 35B was the ultimate version, with a 2.3-litre engine fed by a supercharger. In 1926 it was capable of reaching 125mph, and in that year it won the World Championship. By the end of the 1920s Bugattis had won more races – including the first Monaco Grand Prix – than any other manufacturer, and Type 35Bs were credited with winning an average of 14 races per week! The Type 35 was developed into the 51, with twin overhead cams and yet more power, but by that time German teams ruled the Grand Prix roost.

Today, the Type 35B is one of the world's most valuable cars – and if you've seen one racing, you'll know why. The music of the unsilenced straight eight, overlaid with the high-pitched scream of the supercharger, is never forgotten. In its day, it was described as 'tearing calico'. In reality, it's the sound of mechanical genius.

Specifications

Production dates	1926-1928
Manufactured units	45
Engine type	Straight 8 supercharged
Engine size	2,262cc
Maximum power	138bhp
Transmission	4-speed
Top speed	125mph
0-60 mph time	N/A
Country of origin	France

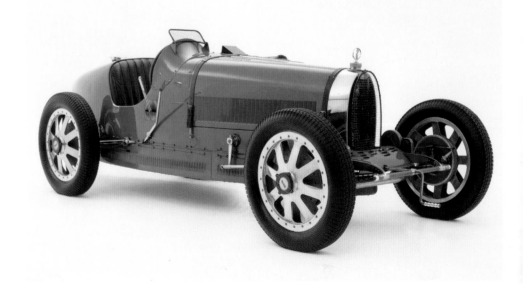

'The Type 35 and 35B Bugattis were phenomenally successful competition cars. In the late 1920s it was said that they averaged 14 race wins per week!'

The last word in 1930s bespoke engineering

The 'best cars in the world' came about through the partnership of engineer Henry Royce and salesman Charles Rolls. Their 40/50 model of 1906, known as the Silver Ghost, was certainly worthy of this accolade: the famously silent Ghost was made right up until 1926, with many built at their US factory in Springfield, Massachusetts.

During the Great War, Rolls-Royce had begun to built V12 aero engines, though it was not until

Rolls-Royce Phantom III

1936 that this configuration of engine would appear in one on their cars. This meant that neither Royce nor Rolls were to see this ultimate development of their car: Rolls was the first Englishman to die in an air crash in 1910 and Royce died in 1933.

In 1926 came the Phantom I, with a new overhead valve 7,668cc six-cylinder engine. For 1929 it evolved into the Phantom II. There was also a smaller 20hp model, which developed into the 20/25 and the 25/30. It was the Phantom III, however, that was to be the pinnacle of pre-WW2 automotive engineering.

The aircraft and ship engines produced by Rolls-Royce were a major influence on the engine of the PIII, a 7,340cc overhead valve V12. Cadillac had tried to go one up with a V16, but it was a simple

side-valve device, and not in the same engineering league as the PIII. The advantages of the V12 layout were sublime smoothness and considerable power: Rolls-Royce were always coy about power outputs, simply stating that they were 'adequate'. In fact, the V12 made something like 170bhp, which was more than adequate.

The PIII also had far more modern suspension than its predecessors. The independent front suspension used coil springs and wishbones, as developed by General Motors.

Unsurprisingly, the PIII was expensive. Not until after the war did RR build their own bodies, so having purchased the chassis a person then had to take it to their favourite coachbuilder. In the US, a complete car would have cost around $15,000 – the same amount that would have bought five Cadillac 75s!

Hostilities of 1939 halted production, which meant that the V12 never reached its development potential, and the era of hand-built bespoke engineering came to a close.

Incidentally, a Phantom III should never be referred to as a 'Rolls': any pre-war Rolls-Royce is more appropriately referred to as a 'Royce'.

Specifications

Production dates	1936-1939
Manufactured units	710
Engine type	V12, pushrod operated overhead valve
Engine size	7,340cc
Maximum power	170bph
Transmission	4-speed synchromesh
Top speed	Approx 92mph
0-50 mph time	N/A
Country of origin	UK

The inimitable Bug has the strangest and longest story of any motor car in history

On July 30th, 2003, Beetle number 21,529,464 left the Puebla factory in Mexico. It was the very last one. The story of the world's most successful car had started an incredible 70 years earlier – and it's one of the most remarkable in the business.

Hitler is often credited with inventing the Beetle, but it wasn't really so. The idea came from Dr Ferdinand Porsche, and was brought to Hitler's attention in 1933, the year that he became

VW Beetle

chancellor. It was on June 22, 1934 that Porsche secured a contract to build a prototype for the 'people's car'.

There is much discussion over who contributed what to the design, but Czech Hans Ledwinka, from the Tatra company, is thought by some to have had much to do with it. By 1934 there was also a very Beetle-esque rear-engine Mercedes on the market.

With assistance from Mercedes Benz, three cars were built in 1936, and a further 30 pre-production cars in 1937. In 1938, Hitler laid the foundation stone of the factory near Hanover where the car was to be built. It was to be called the 'KdF-Wagen', or, 'strength through joy car'. The new factory spent the war making weapons and military vehicles, but in 1945 the tooling for the KdF-Wagen had survived.

The factory, and the town built to service it, ended up under the jurisdiction of the British Military Government, which at first failed to realise quite what it had. A young Major Ivan Hirst was appointed to sort out the factory, which had last been used to build rockets with slave labour, and which had been badly bombed. Hirst saw the potential, and persuaded the military police to place an order for 20,000 vehicles. He scrounged steel and supplies, and by 1946, 1,000 cars a month were being built. In 1949, the renamed Wolfsburg town and factory were handed over to the new West German government.

VW promoted the little car in the US, and against all preconceptions the Americans took the Bug to their heart, buying them in their millions.

The tiny 1,131cc engine grew in size and power, while the split rear window became one, and got bigger. Eventually, the windscreen became curved and the torsion bar front suspension gave way to modern struts. And yet the Beetle's character never really changed.

In 1972, it overtook the Model T Ford's record for production numbers, and it seems unlikely that any car will ever exceed the VW's 21.5 million examples built over its 57 years.

Specifications

Production dates	1946-2003
Manufactured units	21,529,464
Engine type	Flat 4, air-cooled, rear-mounted
Engine size	1131cc-1584cc
Maximum power	25bhp-50bhp
Transmission	4-speed synchromesh
Top speed	62mph-82mph
0-60 mph time	17.1 seconds (1303-1584cc)
Country of origin	Germany

'...against all preconceptions the Americans took the Bug to their heart, buying them in their millions'

For the T-Bird, first was best, as the purity of the two-seater cars was never fully recaptured

It was Chevrolet that made the Thunderbird happen. In 1953, it brought out the Corvette, and GM certainly weren't going to have anything that Ford didn't have. Ford wanted a more practical vehicle than the 'Vette, so, rather than calling the T-Bird a sports car, it termed its new creation a 'personal' car.

The T-Bird fused low-slung elegance with a thoroughly Ford look. It was not the out-and-out

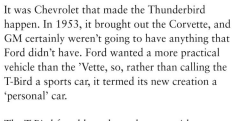

'55-'57 Ford Thunderbird

got the no-cost option of distinctive portholes in the hard top. Remember the mystery girl's white T-Bird in 'American Graffiti'?

For 1957 there was a light makeover, with a different bumper and grill, and a longer rear deck for more trunk space. Elegance was undiminished, and you could now get up to 285bhp if you ticked the right boxes. They even went racing with a 340bhp supercharged version – only 208 were built, and success was limited.

sports car that the early Corvette had tried and failed to be. It sat on the same 102in wheelbase, but there were proper wind-up windows, a power top and a lift-off hard top. Under the hood was a beefy 193bhp Mercury V8, while the 'Vette struggled with flappy side screens and a limp six pot. Under that gorgeous skin it might have run on standard Ford parts from lesser models in the range, but who cared?

On release in 1955 it was priced at an irresistible $3,000, and as a result managed to outsell the Corvette that year by an incredible 24 to one.

Detroit restyled its models every season in the 1950s, but the runaway success of the T-Bird meant that it was too good to change. For 1956 it received a 'continental' spare wheel on the back, a little more power and softer suspension. It also

Ford wanted greater sales, and for 1958 the T-Bird became a four seater. The new car was so ugly that even its mother couldn't have loved it, but the American public did, and it sold twice as well as the two-seater cars had.

The T-Bird would never be a two-seater again, but the 1961 to 1963 cars regained a beauty and simplicity of line, and would later feature in the film 'Thelma and Louise'.

The 1964 model held on to some of its predecessors' looks, but from there on it was downhill all the way, with the T-Bird becoming a car for men wearing white shoes and plaid slacks.

Specifications

Production dates	1955-1957
Manufactured units	53,166
Engine type	V8 pushrod OHV
Engine size	4,785cc; 5,112cc
Maximum power	193bhp-285bhp
Transmission	3-speed manual with optional overdrive, or 3-speed automatic
Top speed	105mph-125mph
0-60 mph time	11.5-7.0 seconds
Country of origin	USA

'...the runaway success of the T-Bird meant that it was too good to change'

The DB Astons were the epitome of the post-war sports car, with exceptional lines and success on the track

Aston Martin got its name from the English village of Aston Clinton, where Lionel Martin had competed in hill climbs. The first Aston Martin appeared in 1914, and in 1921 came racing success at the Brooklands track. The company built small-engined, hand-made sports cars that were very special, but very expensive. It first went bust in 1924, and from then on was always on a shaky financial footing.

Aston Martin DB4/DB5

In 1947, the company was bought by tractor magnate David Brown. A four-cylinder engine had been designed, but Brown wanted more. He had also purchased Lagonda, and with it came a twin overhead cam six-cylinder unit, which had been designed by the great W.O Bentley, and was used to power his Astons.

The DB2 of 1949 was a sleek coupé along the lines of Ferraris at the time. Rather confusingly, it developed to become the DB2/4, DB2/4 Mk II, and the DB Mk III. The DB3 was a sports racing car, as were the DB3S and the DBR 1, which won both Le Mans and the World Sports Car Championship for David Brown in 1959.

The DB4 in 1958 was all new, including its engine, designed by Polish engineer Tadek

Marek. It was another twin-cam six, but larger at 3,670cc. It was claimed to make 240bhp, and to give the DB4 a top speed of 140mph, both claims that may have been a little enthusiastic.

The styling was svelte and lithe, and the unique bodywork was handmade using the 'superleggera', or 'super light', technique of Carrozzeria Touring of Milan.

In 1962 there came a convertible. There was a faster Vantage version, and a very fast short wheelbase DB4 GT. Then there were 19 GTs with beautiful bodies built by Zagato in Italy.

In 1963 the DB4 became the DB5. It used the faired-in lights of the GT, but looked little different to the DB4. The engine was enlarged to 3,995cc and there was 282bhp available. The DB6 in 1965 was a heavier, less elegant motor car.

The DB5 shot to worldwide fame when Sean Connery's James Bond drove one in 'Goldfinger'. The Corgi toy sold in millions to small boys, and although they're all grown up, for most of them the DB5 remains as unattainable as ever.

Specifications

Production dates	1958-1963 (DB4); 1963-1965 (DB5)
Manufactured units	1,110 (DB4); 1,021 (DB5)
Engine type	Twin-cam 6-cylinder
Engine size	3,670cc (DB4); 3,995cc (DB5)
Maximum power	240bhp (DB4); 285bhp (DB5); 315bph (DB4 Zagato)
Transmission	4-speed sychromesh
Top speed	140mph+
0-60 mph time	8.1 seconds
Country of origin	UK

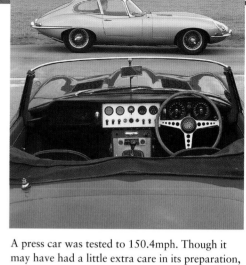

America loved it so much that they bought most of them. No export has done more for Britain's image than the E-Type Jag

Few cars have caused a storm like the one at the unveiling of the E-Type in 1961. The XK120 of 1948 had been cutting edge, but by now it had developed into the XK150 and was fairly antiquated. With a heavy separate chassis it was tall and old-fashioned. Its replacement could not have been more different.

Jaguar had been extremely successful in sports-car racing during the 1950s, with Le Mans victories

Jaguar E-Type

in 1951, 1953, and 1955 through to 1957. First there had been the C-Type, with the brand new technology of disc brakes. Then came the D-Type with its aerodynamic form and unitary chassis. All the lessons learnt at the La Sarthe track were used in the design of the E-Type.

There were Dunlop disc brakes all round, and the body was of unitary, or monocoque, construction. This allowed it to be low, and it's hard to think of a car that looks lower than the E-Type. It plainly owed much to the lines of the D-Type, but that was a racing car and didn't have to sell. The E-Type shared the same small oval grill and faired-in lights, but it was styled to please – and please it did. The roadster and the fixed-head coupé vied to be the most beautiful car in the world.

A press car was tested to 150.4mph. Though it may have had a little extra care in its preparation, customers' cars could get very close to this magic number. The same car reached 60 in 6.9 seconds.

It wasn't just fast and beautiful. With sophisticated independent rear suspension it handled well and rode like no sports car before it. This was a car in which to cross continents.

The E-Type had one more trump card up its sleeve – it was cheap. Jags had always been good value, and combined with great performance, this had created a slightly unwelcome image. A derogatory term for the middle classes was 'the Jag and gin brigade'. All this was forgotten with the E-Type – it was just too good to knock.

Its unique combination of qualities mean the E-Type will never go out of fashion, yet even now it's remarkable value next to an Aston or Ferrari.

Specifications

Production dates	1961-1973 (all types)
Manufactured units	72,584 (all types)
Engine type	6-cylinder twin overhead cam
Engine size	3,781cc (pre-1964)
Maximum power	265bhp
Transmission	4-speed sychromesh
Top speed	150mph
0-60 mph time	7.1 seconds
Country of origin	UK

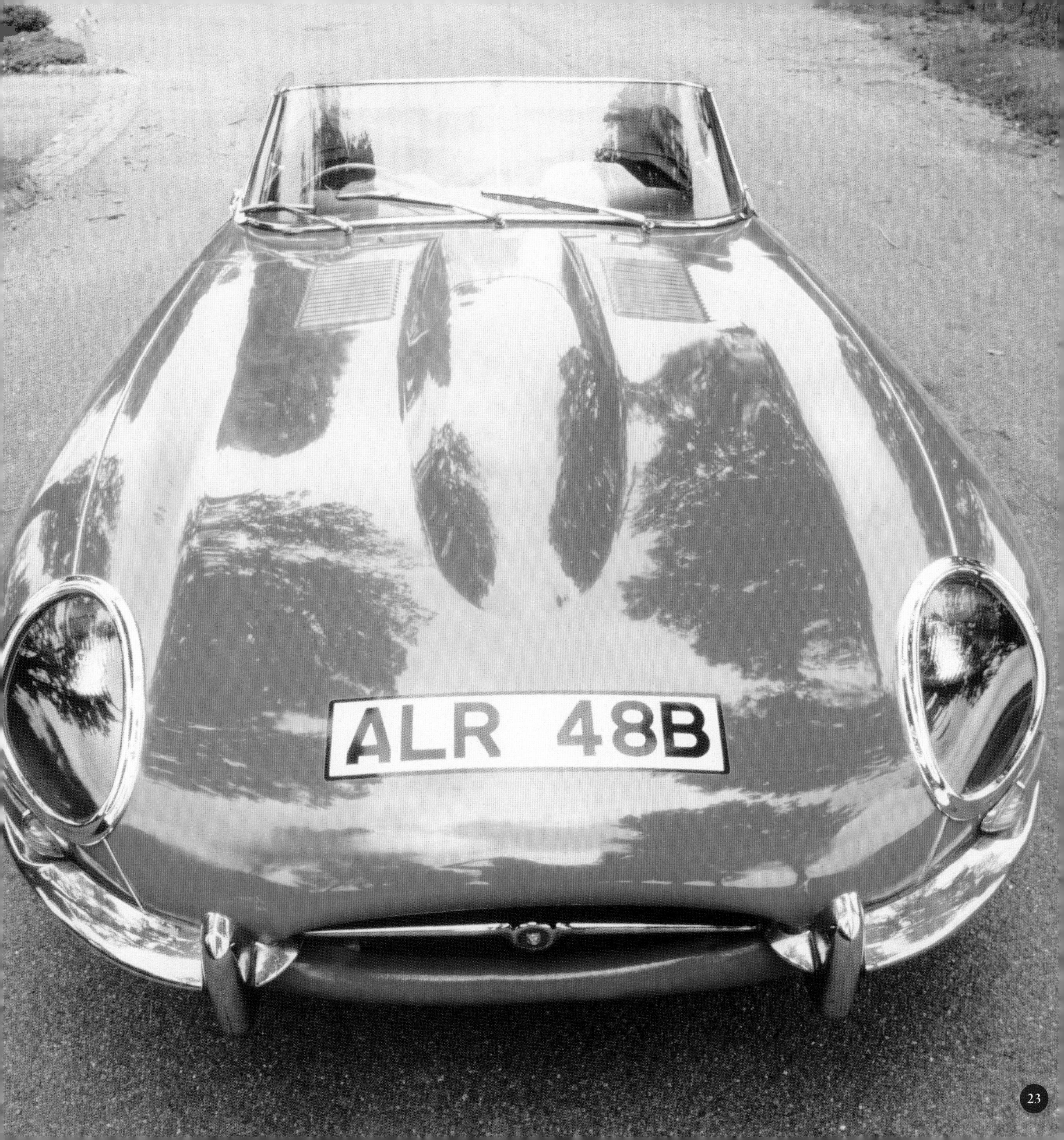
ALR 48B

The MGB was a sports car for every man. The MGB GT was a sports car for every man and his dog

Ever since the end of WW2, MG seem to have been selling old-fashioned cars to old-fashioned people. With the release of the MGB in 1962, that was to change – at least for a while.

The MGA had been a direct development of the T series cars, with their pre-war roots. In spite of this, it was too modern for many British sports-car enthusiasts – who would have been shocked by its replacement, the thoroughly modern B.

MGB

The B was of monocoque construction. This wasn't exactly ground breaking, but the Austin-Healey and Triumph opposition were still built on separate chassis. The mechanical bits came from the rather mundane Austin and Morris saloons. The B series engine was tuned to 95bhp and that meant 100mph. It was enough to make the B an instant bestseller.

In 1965 came a coupé version with small back seats. The clever bit was an opening rear hatch, considerably pre-dating the hatchback boom. The MGB GT's back seats weren't very useful, but there was plenty of room for the dog and the shopping. Practicality meant excellent sales.

By the 1970s, the B was long in the tooth, and MG were back to selling simple outdated cars to those who could not embrace modernity. In

1974, the disastrous decision was made to fit all MGBs with the US spec 5mph impact bumpers. The MGB became a bit of a joke – in fact, with hindsight, the rubber bumper cars drive almost identically to earlier cars, but they do look awful.

Management indifference and incompetence meant that no successor to the B was developed, and, with complete inevitability, the MG factory closed in 1980.

There had been interesting variations on the MGB theme, but none were properly developed or marketed. The MGC of 1967 was powered by a modernised version of the 3.0-litre Healey's engine. Unfortunately, it was underpowered, and the great weight of the engine ruined the B's tidy handling. The MGB GT V8 of 1973 was much better. The lightweight Rover V8 meant 125mph and 0 to 60 in just 8 seconds, but only 2,591 of these misunderstood coupés were made.

It's no road burner, but as a sports car to live with, the B still takes some beating.

Specifications

Production dates	1962-1980
Manufactured units	365,000 (MGB); 150,000 (MGB GT)
Engine type	4-cylinder push rod OHV
Engine size	1,798cc
Maximum power	95bhp
Transmission	4-speed sychromesh, optional overdrive, optional automatic – avoid!
Top speed	105mph
0-60 mph time	12.1 seconds
Country of origin	UK

For some, too much is never enough.
The Cobra is the car for them

AC (which stands for Autocarriers), had been building cars in Thames Ditton, south of London, since 1904. After WW2, they resumed production by putting the six-cylinder engine they had been making since 1921 into a rather ungainly saloon. Things improved when they adopted a design by John Tojeiro, based rather closely on the contemporary Ferrari Barcetta. This was the AC Ace of 1954, and as well as fitting their own engine, AC also used Bristol and Ford units later

AC Cobra

on. The Ace, particularly with Bristol power, was quick, good looking, and handled a treat.

In 1961, Bristol stopped making their engine, preferring to utilise the easy power of an American V8, and AC soon followed suit.

Texan racing driver Carroll Shelby fitted a Ford V8 to an Ace, and the rest, as they say, is history. Starting with a 4.2-litre, it was soon the 4.7, or 289 cubic inch, that was used. The old chassis coped manfully with twice the power it was designed for.

Even the 350bhp that the 289 could be persuaded to push out wasn't enough, and Shelby set about squeezing in the 7.0-litre 427 big block. This time, some big changes were needed to give the chassis a fighting chance. The antiquated transverse leaf springs were gone in favour of wishbones and coils. The chassis tubes were also enlarged.

The 289 was an animal, but the 427 was a monster. To accommodate much fatter rubber, the

wheel arches were widened, giving the appearance of a body builder's biceps. No car has ever looked tougher, or had more muscle to back it up. If the 425bhp of the standard 427 wasn't quite enough, you could order up a 485. 'Motor' magazine tested such a car, accelerating to 100mph in a phenomenal 10.1 seconds!

There was success on the track, as one might expect, and there were several beautiful Daytona coupés built just for racing.

No car has been as copied as the 427 Cobra, its brutish good looks making it irresistible to kit car builders. And yet, opinions divulge wildly. There are those who say that the Cobra's chassis could never really cope, making the handling twitchy and difficult. Amongst the acolytes there are also those who say it's the most overrated car in history. Unfortunately, few of us will ever have the chance to find out.

Specifications

Production dates	1962-1969
Manufactured units	560 (289); 510 (427)
Engine type	V8 pushrod OHV
Engine size	4,727cc (289); 6,997cc (427)
Maximum power	270bhp-485bhp
Transmission	4-speed manual
Top speed	160mph
0-60 mph time	4.6 seconds (427)
Country of origin	UK, engine USA

'If imitation really is the sincerest form of flattery, then the Cobra should be the greatest car of all time. Fibreglass kit car replicas have made the shape familiar, but it's still a fabulous-looking car'

Ferruccio's Miura set the standard for supercars, and remains the most beautiful in perpetuity

In 1961 there was something of a walkout at Ferrari. Enzo was infamous for his conservatism. He had, for instance, resisted using British-invented disc brakes to the point where his cars looked ridiculous. Frustration at their inability to realise their ideas led to the departure of six of 'Il Comendatore's' top designers and engineers.

There were unhappy customers as well. One was Ferruccio Lamborghini. Producing tractors and

Lamborghini Miura

air-conditioning systems had made him wealthy, and now he decided to beat Enzo at his own game. Ford were to do just that on the race track, but Lamborghini was only interested in building a better road car.

Giotto Bizzarrini, who had designed the immortal Ferrari 250 GTO, designed a fabulous new engine for Lamborghini. Ferrari used a single cam per bank of their V12; his V12 would have two. This wonderful four-cam engine powered the first Lamborghini, the 350GT, which was unveiled in 1963. It was technically what Bizzarrini had wanted the GTO to be, but the styling was a

little dubious and sales were disappointing. A similar 400GT followed, but it was in 1966 that Ferruccio staked a genuine claim on immortality.

His engineers still wanted to go racing. The mid-engined layout was now ubiquitous on the track, but the length of the V12 engine was a problem. Dallara and the other Ferrari renegades came up with the brilliant idea of placing the engine transversely, across the car behind the driver. Ferruccio said, 'Great, but we're not going racing – make it a road car'.

Design house Bertone were keen to come on board, as rivals Pininfarina were cosy with Ferrari. The young and ambitious Macello Gandini was given the job and penned the most flowing and sensuous lines that would ever be seen on a mid-engined car.

The Miura P400 took the 1966 Geneva Motor Show by storm. It was technical marvel, with the engine block, gearbox, and final drive all made in one complex casting. It performed as good as it looked, completely rewriting the sports-car rules.

There followed a more powerful S model, and the ultimate SV in 1971, capable of over 170mph. In 1974 the Countach took over. It was shocking and sensational, but it wasn't beautiful.

What a shame that the nearest most of us will come to driving a Miura is watching the opening sequence of 'The Italian Job'.

Specifications

Production dates	1966-1972
Manufactured units	765
Engine type	V12 4-cam, transverse rear-mounted
Engine size	3,929cc
Maximum power	350bhp (SV 385bhp)
Transmission	5-speed in unit with engine
Top speed	171mph
0-60 mph time	5.5 seconds
Country of origin	Italy